> "Look to the Moon if you are lost,
>
> She holds all power"
>
> – *Kayleigh Mickayla Mooney*

Copyright 2019 © All Rights Reserved. Kayleigh Mickayla Mooney and Kevin Michael Mooney.

For any permissions, including to use or copy, in part or in whole, please contact <u>clemys@sbcglobal.net</u> or <u>kmmlaw12@gmail.com</u>.

978-0-578-63028-1

A Preamble: The Ministry of Presence

We have always been present with each other. For centuries. I was there with you, miraculously, on that night, and thank God. You are now here with me, ministering to your Father. Your Mother. Your Brother. Holding our hands. A ministry of presence.

You, in the physical, were a perfectly happy, healthy child. Vibrant beyond the normal fifteen year old; battle tested, witty, hilarious, artistic, beautiful, dynamic, brilliant, filled with compassion and love. Your ocean blue eyes conjured wisdom and God's light, swirling about in practical manners; a young woman who could hear the sea, feel the sea, know the sea. The spirit of the sea speaks to the soul, and it always spoke to and always speaks to you.

We never missed a day together. We have not missed a day since that moment that changed everything. A week earlier, on vacation on the Atlantic, I saw you standing eye to eye level with me in a black bikini and thought, 'she has finally arrived; my child woman, my little girl is a woman.' I could not wait for tenth grade beginning in a week, and the years after, charging into adulthood, watching you take on the world and becoming even more beautiful and wise.

A week later, in an innocent instant, a vibrant and happy young woman on a stagnant August night, you were blindsided by a car while attempting simply to cross a busy street. Your only desire was to come home to kiss me on my forehead; to take a night walk with Mommy; to play VR with your little Brother. That was it. Now the grief nearly suffocates my soul. For brevity, only a fraction of grief can be captured here. Only fractional beauty is harnessed in these lyrics, for nothing so much minimizes the pulsing language of the soul than trying to describe it in human words.

I was there with you, miraculously, within minutes. In that moment in the street, while holding you in the cradle of my soul, my arms, my voice; a holy orb of light surrounded us, to be penetrated by none. Locked into each other's souls, you listened to your Father tell you he loves you, that he was right there beside you, that you would be okay. And you, trusting me beyond all others, blossomed into the fullest authentic faith one can manage; and seeing the light of God, seeing the distant beaches, you pressed forward and passed right through my physical body, emerging on my right side, wholly empowered in your body of light, holding me firmly, your left shoulder against my right shoulder, looking down with me at your beautiful body lying in the street.

For Mommy and Daddy made your physical body. Yet we did not make your soul. That was God's work. As your physical body died, your life simply transitioned into your illuminated body of light, an angel, a thousand times stronger now than you had been before the accident. In that moment in the street, as you took your last breath and wreathed around me, you opened a magnificent window and tried to show me a glimpse of Heaven – an infinite, luminous beach of pure light and love.

Our Heaven is many things. Since your transition, you have scouted out our most perfect Heaven, the glory of the Higher Life, "*Exuma Infinite.*" You are scouting out diving sites and beaches to walk upon. You take me there when I can raise my vibration high enough, though still tethered to my human body, and for each day moving forward, reconciling and struggling with immeasurable grief. You dance there, skipping stars across the turquoise water. You live there, as you live here, on both sides of the veil, a guardian angel protecting and leading her family home, home to a beautiful world where this beach glows pristinely in its immortality. Kayleigh, I love you so…

OF EXITING INTO EXUMA

"The Obedience of Light"

The way you locked your soul into my soul,
The way you locked your soul into God,
Laying in the street,
A total obedience of light,
Focused on your Fathers,
As you passed from life to life,
Focused on your Fathers,
As you walked into The Light.

"Awaiting Her Father on the Sands of Exuma Infinite"

Skipping stars across the surface of the turquoise ocean,
She holds tiny stones of fire in her palms,
They spark, bouncing across the waters until they dip below horizon,
And lower torpid waves into a tranquil calm.

"The Mighty Atlantic"

Yet find me as but man,
Mortal contraband,
Skinned in delicate human shell,
So easily expelled...

...You rage, storming ocean stirs,
And waves, emotionally disturbed,
Throw their weight upon the land,
Exploding into well abused sand,
And leaving its mark,
A long jagged line of seaweed scar,
That tells the tale of its mighty rant...

...Yet I am as you found me,
Just a simple man,
Human freight,
Cellular contraband,
Yet be not confused as I am also a soul,
That can hold you in its hand...

...Oh mighty Atlantic,
I thought it important that you understand...

"Nothing Will Stop This Father..."

Leaning into the natural forces of total destruction,
Walking fiercely, directly through the chaotic maelstrom of a hurricane,
The texture of this beast - it ranges through my blood,
It flattens my bones in the torrent,
As I strain every life that has come before,
To be with you -

Not knowing the direction, visually,
Through the cyclical blades of wind,
Instead, I close these human eyes and follow the eternal vision of the soul,
Through the howling, deafening roar,
And I see you there off in the sunlight, on our pleasant beach, on the other side,
With turquoise waters and purple sky,
Radiating with joy and love and encouragement and pride,
And you see me here in the spinning sheets of this storm,
Fighting toward you,
With the love of a father blazing in my eyes,
That no hurricane resists,
No hurricane defies.

"One Hour"

One hour without you is like a month without breath,
An ocean without water,
One hour without my daughter,
A night that never sets,
A day that never rises,
A thousand, thousand deaths,
One hour, you are centuries,
To claw through with barren voice upset,
A bird without wings,
And sleep without rest,
Air with no oxygen,
A life without breath.

"A Metal Boat upon a Steel River"

The friction of a metal boat floating on a steel river,
Scraping along with sparks that mark the skin that pocks and shivers,
Yet grief, it flows, it fuels the engine,
A wayward map without a legend,
It flows wherever it wants to flow...

...Crashing through the chamber doors where God's blinding light shines,
The angels thread their wings together to hold back the tides...

...Hush...

He lay quietly, like a baby, cradled by keel and ribs,
For the thief cannot take that which he gives,
Above him, blue purple smoke laces through black clouds,
Its fabric hangs across the air like Celtic crosses posted in the ground,
Copper rust rains from lucid, acrid skies,
Like spiked chlorine that strikes his skin and beds his eyes,
And burns the valleys where the virgin soil sleeps...

...And the rains have come, but the rains will go,
And he grips the oar and with a mighty blow,
He strikes the metal river and propels himself forward,
Just a few feet more...

"This Clay Charade"

Darkness burns holes in the distance,
Darkness crows - it sparks - it barks,
Darkness crowns resistance,
As legends rip the map apart,
Yet it fueled me with persistence,
That led to the center of your heart,
I now find my way with blindness as my guide,
In the realm where no vision hides,
I see with blistered hands of friction,
And ears bent towards dereliction,
Listening for footsteps to trespass upon this yard,
And walk upon this clay charade,
It is harder than it is hard,
No life should confront such egregious pain,
That no life can disregard...

...Today.

"Black Metallic Rain"

Awash in the sky clouded deep metal gray,
With black sheets of rain that flood the terrain,
The pools - silver mirrors, reflecting the terrors that haunt me -

The showers like daggers of old rusty nails,
That slice through emotion when the defenses fail,
And crash and recoil - and rip through the soils that cage me -

What weather is this with its grim atmosphere,
Where the mixture of pain blends with sadness and fear,
And anger and angst and the danger at lengths comes to taunt me -

But there is no shelter - no means of escape,
So I stand in the storm and scream in its face,
And suffer and struggle - releasing the strain that will save me -

The trees and the fields and the valleys hang in black,
With a stale soup of tar that oozed from earth's back,
I wipe the ink from my eyes, these terrible skies…

…And rekindle…

"To Die One Hundred Times a Day"

Forced by the tether, trudging perilous road,
The leather skins of a cobra cover the heels like coats,
With hairline fractures like poppy bruises blotch my shins,
I plod forward and the ankles pop - and eyes turn within;

With the soul of a warrior and the cunning of a wolf,
With a fierce dedication, and a self-sacrificing pulse,
I collapse onto kneecaps - I wipe from brow the ugly trace,
Of the grief that comes to wrestle the last light in my face,
But know I am coming, over fields and hills and lands,
I am coming, my Darling, just to hold your hands;

Pressing forth and the earthly air like glassy pumice in my chest,
Slices like obsidian blades each time the breath expressed,
But never mind, mind not, for I shall not be kept away,
The light of my love for you shines brighter,
Than my death one hundred times a day.

"A Century, a Second"

It takes a century to track the life of a second,
In those moments,
A century of living, with all of its lessons,
As if time was frozen,
As the soul itself exerts,
Itself,
And the in- breath, for out, reverts,
Into the next second,
Tied together one by one,
Into hours chained like metal tears into the necklace of a day,
And another into others into a month,
That scavenged its way,
Across the broken ground,
And evolved across these earths into one year,
And another,
Vacant of scent and sound.

"In the Salty Fields"

Dream, drift and seethe,
On the oceans like fallen tree forsaken,
Weep in the caldron of the sea,
In the salty fields until you have awaken,
And beached in a quiet dereliction,
Exhausted by experience afloat,
And skinned raw red by the friction,
And grief that has you by the throat,
Flaunts your dismal weakened condition,
And taunts you in its deliberate goad,
To subjugate to its religion,
And toss you back into the tidal folds,
Until the salty fields,
Have claimed you as their own.

"The Sand Here, Daddy"

Daddy, the sand is like pillows,
Like pillows cradling your feet,
It shines like the sun and sighs,
It radiates when it sees that you believe,
It is as alive as you and I are,
Regardless of your grief,
It is like the beach is packed with a billion stars,
That pause to give you relief...

...The sand here, Daddy,
It is beautiful,
Like nothing before you have ever seen...

"Metal Breath"

And breathe, burning oxygen in lungs,
Like sweat, the gummy smell that rakes the tongue,
Leaves its sour smell within the mouth,
Of all of the pain that couldn't find its way out -

And seethe, oozing grief pressed to the skin,
Like yellow blood that foments into silvery tin,
It clings, like oily viscous grime,
With a crust that flakes of atomic #29 -

...She, lay seedlings of dreams in the soul,
That burst into flower fields of green and blue and gold,
Scented with a heavenly, minty fruit,
That forces out the metal in this earthly pursuit.

"Mystery Galaxy"

Light sparked, chafed by particles of dust,
Heated by the stars as they birthed and combust,
Forming and growing inside a galaxy,
Layering light like waves upon the sea,
But the blush of dust clouds themselves,
Obscure these birthing stars within its stew,
Which make the galaxy itself invisible from our view;

This is the miracle of life,
The mystery of the Universal Light,
A massive monster galaxy with as many stars as our Milky Way,
Yet hidden in the folds of space,
Brimming with activity, new stars are formed,
At one hundred times the rate of our own,
Yet hidden from our eyes,
As our greatest telescopes range the skies...

...There are lush sparkling gardens of beaches, illumination pressed by angels' feet,
She plays there when she wishes,
Upon these swirling golden seas...

...It is an outpost of love, on the outskirts of memory,
She prepares a spectacular beachfront there,
As she awaits her family...

"Celestial Silvery Dawn"

She, the Ancient, the great eternal soul,
Illuminates the darkness that midnight claimed to hold,
Dancing fires that glitter atop the fields of ocean foam,
Reflects her majesty in each wave's pitch and roll,
She tucks the night time clasped within her hold,
Lighting up the beachfront with her great celestial glow,
She is promise - that one day we shall know,
The dawn of the heavens - and its eternal gold.

"For At the Sea the Vibration is Higher"

In near silence the voice of the sea,
Speaks to the soul - and so clearly,
Tales of its mysteries,
Are given to those who believe,
And I believe in you -

...And liquid light pulses through these sky fields,
These frontiers of golden country where the spirit reveals,
Its truth -

...I was there awaiting, anticipating,
Your presence - your lovely entrance,
I sensed a shift in the doorway,
Lilac flavored and Lavender scented,
Reminded me of the gardens of your youth,
And running down the path in flip flops,
And falling and chipping a tooth -

...And there I was, always with embrace,
Wiping the tears from your face,
And tiny blonde locks from your eyes,
My Love...

Now as this cage looms to age me early,
With the tragedy that bucks and chokes and disturbs me,
And challenges me to rise and rise again,
I know an intuitive trick in the balance,
And a vow that I will always defend,
You are always present - it is I - when in grief,
That blocks me from your whispers,
And the words that you speak,
That leaves me feeling helpless though you are picking up my feet,
The vibration is higher when we are walking at the sea.

"Seconds on the Road of a Lifetime"

A long, stretched out single second slowly groans,
Packed with heartache, grief and pain that makes a moment swollen full,
With little room for life,
Though I am left with this very plight,
For I must press against the lifetime sentence,
That thrives within each every second...

...To open up a sacred road.

"My Love Song to You"

My love song to you is simply my life,
The days ahead,
The flows and ebbs,
The gardens tending,
Wounds amending,
Through the triumph and the strife,
My love song to you is how I treat my life -

A thieving grievance bites to shun me,
A forbearance scores my earth,
A poison fills the lowlands and leads to my sea,
I will tend to that also because,
My Love, you see,
My love song is the condition of my life,
To which I have bequeathed,
My gift of me to you -

I will not leave this human skin,
Leaving a debris field of my country within,
Leaving a wretched wreck on the shores of your soul,
No, no - I will not dishonor you,
I will offer you light, and love to behold,
By churning my spirit into luminous gold,
By each step that I take here,
With intention - with this goal,
I write my love song to you,
As we walk the remainder of my road.

"Walking on Mars"

Spread through the vigil of veritable night,
The seeds of sunrise sprout in blaze of first flailing light,
They spring from your palms and spread like a green sea of life;

You hold the words that flesh in this song,
You know the world has done us a wrong,
A wrong for which forgiveness is barred,
A horrible accident and now, here we are -

I spun the wheels to turn back the time,
Held my breath to hear the meaning divine,
I stared at the trees until their faces of leaves fell upon me -

I took an audience with our beautiful Lord,
Peppered Him with questions like I was swinging a sword,
I fell to my knees and lashed at Him for responding -

I have screamed - I have cried,
Thrown a spear down its throat,
Tied off its venom with a snare and a rope,
And slept in its vomit like a blanket of moons and of stars -

I have died nearly one thousand deaths,
In each cresting peak of each painful breath,
Wept in the company of loneliness like I was walking on Mars -

Yet this path continues until these eyes come to rest,
As I walk the red planet with medals pinned to my chest,
For I am a warrior with laurels from campaigns and conquest -

Though this is not true it's not far from the truth,
For I am a warrior in what I pursue,
A Daddy, in grieving, reaching across just to touch you.

"An Olive Shell"

Oliva Sayana - shattered of bone,
Like a butterfly is crushed by stone,
Its pieces dance in the waves,
Across the range of sea graves,
Where the dust of their lives,
Settle into the beach's changing face;

She picks up my scarred and torn shell,
Brushes off the scorched marks from the fires of hell,
And throws me on her back,
Nearly lifeless, bewitched of fact,
My wounded frame, my wounded heart, my wounded soul,
And walked across the debris field of my life,
With only one goal…

…To safely guide me home.

"Sky Road"

With a pioneering spirit,
A guardian soul,
And a passion for your family,
You closely hold,
You are charting beacons in the heavens,
Torches of love - torches aglow,
Planting them in the darkness of night,
Fire flowers, spectacles of gold,
A path, an arch to go over,
Illuminated by the light of the stars,
You have placed along the Sky Road,
For loved ones,
For loved ones to find their way home.

"A Lifeboat Planked in Poetry"

Muse, your music - it dances on the tongue,
You were stolen from my earthly presence,
Too young,
Both of us - much too young;

Muse, your magic - it harvests the birthing sun,
And brings a million sunrises in the flash of every dawn,
Still, the steps forward from this tragedy are daunting,
My daughter, for which I have called only one;

I am drowning in a sea of traumatic consequence,
When then the poetry - a lifeboat - emerges from the fog,
And offers me the platform of momentary sanctuary,
Just as my breath dips beneath the ebony water,
I hear the lovely chorus of my indigo daughter,
Laying on my heart the offering of her healing song;

My child, please walk in my soul from end to end,
Cleanse me, my fields and streams, the purple hills and heather river bends,
I trust you like no other on this spirit road,
Only one may enter and freely roam my soul,
You, my Muse, we write together the words of my feet,
And hand in hand - and sometimes in your hands, lessening the load,
I find the sacred cradle of your love is the framing of this boat.

"This Forsaken Hero and the Eternity of Now"

This world,
Enslaved with joys and trouble,
So hard at times to unleash, uncouple,
I walked into this paradox with a healthy skepticism,
Where the physical and spiritual hold a mystic rhythm,
I bathed in the rivers of humility,
I gave and gave into the honor of thieves,
I sacrificed all selfish outlook in exchange for the greater good,
For it is in this greatness in which life's mystery,
Could be understood,
Then the world with its random arbitrary sword…

…Destroyed all that I cherished on this God forsaken road -

My child, I hear you when the wind dies down,
I hear you when I lie still on this hallowed ground,
I die one thousand deaths a second,
In each throbbing heart beat I scream and beckon,
For you -

Now you walk with me in your body of light,
My lantern through the dark days now cast in the deepest night,
You speak in language only known to a father and daughter,
Like breathing light that illuminates water,
Your Father searches for the edges to peel back the seam,
Your Father lurches forward in the afterglow of a decadent dream,
For heartache's fingers have gripped my throat,
Though is hasn't seen the fury yet of a father's grief explode -

You are fighting through the barriers of humanity's mesh,
Touching the light body that radiates under my human flesh,
You learn from the highest order of angels,
And convey God's wisdom through aerial angles,
That touch down within this heart...

...I will run through walls of earths for you,
Tear down the barricades of the universe,
Turn the oceans upside down,
And pound the mountains into flattened ground,
As I thrash about at emotional shadows in a violent accord,
Bleed these screams from the acrid pores and soul it seethes,
Fall apart and see the path that melts dimensions somehow,
Like staring into a crystal pool,
Teach me the eternity of now.

"I Looked Tonight To the Sky for Answers"

Black waters above, the endless deep, space,
Encrusted with tiny, distant, silver crystal flakes,
Like little opal lights that flicker,
While drowned in ash and inky lake;

Stringed necklaces of jeweled flame,
Hung in patterns and constellation frames,
Emanate in hopeful, eternal bouquets -

Flowers for the centuries,
Flowers in the angel's hands,
Flowers she disperses to the winds,
As many the beach has grains of sand...

...Their soft, purple petals float back and forth between these two worlds,
And come to rest within my eyes.

"The Night of the Soul"

With the golden promise - dance upon the edge's veil,
And the wind - it carried the dreamer's tail,
As the torch lights lit the night sky's trails,
Through the darkness - singing with a rage of love,
I walk within the safety of her guiding eye...

...If the moon, found crying, let her tears be praised,
She breathes the light of highest life,
In the prayers we practice there is room to stray,
Within this soul - I walk through night,
The darkness night...

...And see the distant rays of distant days...draped in morning light.

"A Bridge to the Everything"

Awash in the labyrinth of grief uninvited,
Like a river of cement that clots,
Tying the soul up into knots,
I choke on the hours of the day -

...And you, you hold the key to break apart the stone,
You will never let me face the darkness alone,
A bridge to the everything,
You are, the intercession, my daughter,
And the guardian of my soul,
You lift my eyes from the road,
A blinding light to which I am exposed,
Sings in your lovely voice...

...And I here you say,

"I am wrapping my wind around you,
I am wrapping my love around you,
Protecting you, Daddy, you,
Wrapping you with my life,
Wrapping you with my arms,
Wrapping you with my light,
Wrapping you with my heart,
Daddy, you, Daddy, you..."

...Between these two worlds I walk towards you,
With the songs of our lives that we sing,
On your bridge of light,
That leads me to the everything.

"Divinity Eyes"

Heartache that owns no description,
It is impossible to convey...

...I long to be captive in the wisdom of your gaze,
To look upon the contours of your beautiful face,
To divine your emotion and guide your teenage days,
My child...

...Your eyes - in photos, videos, daydreams and memories,
They radiate like sparkling fields of aquamarine,
Sea sky sunset washed in indigo hue,
Quartz dipped in sunrise emitting a morning's blue,
I have always seen this beauty in you,
My Love...

...And I propel myself towards you,
In meditation this is clear,
As I lift myself higher,
And shatter the ceiling of this earthly sphere,
I lock my vision directly into your eyes,
Gazing back to me with the mystery of pride,
Knowing that, though I am encased within this human state,
I search endlessly to punch a hole through to the other side,
To band soul to soul,
To hold my child,
To find peace in your Sapphire eyes.

CHANNELING EXUMA

"My Sanctuary"

Will you visit Saturn and take photographs for me,
And then in meditation pass those images to me,
Will you swim the nebula, the ancient solar seas,
Will you mark vacation spots for when I am finally freed,
Will you walk on Titan and leapfrog galaxies,
And whisper tales of miracles within my open dreams...

...While I sleep and as I sleep...

...Will you gather favorite spots into itinerary,
Wherever you want to take me will be my sanctuary.

"An Angel's Delicate Hand in a Distant Nursery"

Liquid purple sky,
Through which golden clusters rise,
Molten smoke - these nurseries,
Spark in her eyes -

Stellar jewels shine,
In rainbow clouds enshrined,
Just listen to the wind,
She has never been more alive -
She cradles infant stars,
In the seas of nebula gas,
Raising the galaxies,
That emerge from Heaven's ash...

...She is watching a million suns rise,
They shine as bright as the love in her eyes.

"In The Moon..."

Shockingly bright,
She is no passive light,
That hangs over the night,
Just pleased with her glow,
Not this one, no -

She is active in flight,
And engaged in this life,
And heals the ways of this soul,
For she lovingly knows...

...The fields of glittering silver that glow upon my sea,
These rivers of stars that flow within me,
Entangled in my galaxies,
That loom in luminescence in her palm -

She is courageous and powerful,
Centuries strong,
She has learned to bridge two worlds and its wound,
She is the glowing reflection of God's own light,
That pools with love's perfection,
And radiates in the moon.

"Green Moon Clouds"

Ethereal veils of spectral velvet,
Crushed mint in effervescent brine,
They hang like regal emerald cloaks,
Across the black, electric sky,
Illuminated in the fury of the heat flash,
When the humid air and the lightning catch,
Spark in the wet heavy fields of thunder rash,
And the haunts of repair,
And a green mist lifts while the rain amassed,
In the storms above the ocean's womb,
Behold the true star - behold the Moon.

"Portal of Light"

Sparkling dust like the moon on the sea,
Not on the glass and not in the trees,
She holds up a lantern,
In the energy gathered,
To show me -

It flickers its way down a corridor of night,
When the air is so still and the silence just right,
She calls for attention,
An intervention,
To hold me -

She waves her hands gently to open the door,
That unveils a glimpse of a magical shore,
But only a keyhole,
How big is this keyhole,
Implore us -

And God has empowered her beautiful life,
To open for us a portal of light,
To show her parents Heaven,
We see flashes of Heaven,
Quick, golden flashes of Heaven,
Before us -

She resonates in the illumination,
Watching our faces beam with elation,
We are here and awake,
In the air - tongues of flame,
In this glory.

"Father Searcher"

I'm lifting up the covers,
For treasures to unfurl,
I'm seeking with my shovels,
Digging up the corners of this world,
Searching through the rubble,
For diamonds, gold and pearls,
But cannot this occasion,
Empty me of words,
Slinging axes in the forest,
To make fields would be absurd,
For some things are impassible,
Yet I rally through the dirt,
For heartache comes to settle in,
For nothing more than this much hurts,
Than grieving for a child,
Than grieving for my girl;

But I will find a pathway through,
And I will find a roadway out,
And I on this occasion,
Am the master of this doubt,
For nothing matters more to me,
Than my children matter more,
And I will build a bridge,
That channels through a door,
And I will claim a mountaintop,
And drop it to its floor,
And I will scale horizons,
Where the air is breathed no more,
For I am here, My Love, for you,
And know exactly what I'm fighting for,
I'm calling out, My Baby,
I'm calling out, oh Lord...

...Then I hear, I hear so vividly,
Though life may blind devoid,
I hear and with proclivity,
And center on your voice,
And vibrantly, I hear this door,
As open as the waves that crash,
And collapse upon my shore...

...It is in this simplicity,
That our souls are deeply moored.

"Black Canvas"

The sky a black canvas,
Devoid of its paint,
Nothing expands this,
Until enters the Saint,
She throws luminescence,
The gold in the green,
Brush strokes with sun's bristles,
Awakens this scene,
A deep royal purple,
A turquoise sea,
White sand and pink clouds,
She paints in my dreams,
And swirls of bold glitter,
And sparkling streams,
And a pathway that offers...

...The deepest journey to me.

"The Intruder"

The intruder lurks unchecked under mask,
And broken screen,
The intruder, framed in open sash,
Prowls the soul along the seams,
The intruder is as familiar as a family member,
Is to me -

It beds down in the conscience and brews its morning tea,
And probes across emotion for signs of fragility,
It scans the mind for weakness, for any entrance it can see,
Whether nightmare or by daytime,
Or through the doorway of a dream -

In the darkness it is stealthy,
This intruder and its greed,
In the darkness it is healthy,
For the fear on which it feeds,
In the darkness I awaken,
To confront elusive thief,
And face him in my hallway,
Armed with faith to fight this grief...

"A Night of the Spirit"

And breathe you will this luscious wind,
The harbor that let the typhoon in,
A silky wave that crests in the sky,
And washes the metal from the eyes;

And stress, it broke and fled in the yield,
Like an army abandoned its wears in the field,
We pick through tents and food and rearm the slaves,
That built the temples and dug the graves;

And in the calm of this new day,
We crawl from the ashes and the disarray,
Cooking breakfast on open fires and we pray,
To be the strength that we dream in the change;

And pain will come, and trail will merge,
With mystic grace after the tempest surge,
She shows the way, she lights the road,
Through the night for the grieving soul.

"Out of the Valleys of Grief"

And God has sent a warrior,
An angel like none other,
On a mission of the ages...

...And this messenger, with bouquets of promises and miracles,
Adorned in sparkling long dresses of light,
She steps through lavender stars,
Through the oil painted doorway of the night,
Laying wreaths, tethered with love and blooming August moon,
In her Father's eyes and on her Mother's womb,
Holding sacred opal candle, flickering,
And can't you see in its flame,
Eternity,
It washes rivers with its oceans,
Like a pool becomes the sea,
These seeds become belief,
As she takes us by our hands,
And leads us out...

...Out of the Valleys of Grief...

"Signs"

As subtle as a hurricane is to the wind,
This one knows the channels where the veil is thin,
She throws the silver glitter, sparked gold and green,
In hopes his soul will see what the eyes fail in dreams -

And vigilance, its own reward,
Mark the find where her spirit soared,
Riddles, speak in tongues to the seeker's ear,
He feels the words when he cannot hear...

...And purple ribbons tied to delicate trees,
Dance among the flora and the rainbow leaves,
They line the path through thickets and stones,
In hopes her Father finds his way back home...

...Pink Saturn, it breathes and rings overflow,
Novas, pulsing orange with transient glow,
A million crystals in the sky path blaze,
Just to catch attention to his wayward gaze...

...And then he sees - and then he felt it,
The signs so plentiful he cannot help it,
She praises him for each tiny gain,
In her way - as subtle as a hurricane!

"A Spirit in its Human Skins"

And though, the limitations vex my desire,
I cross the wilderness and slog through its mire,
Cursed on this plain with matter and time,
Within these skins, and a human mind,
I elevate, though dust clouds strum,
Like buffalo hooves by the millions run,
I cry until my laughter comes,
And glistens, waxed like evening sun.

"Irradiance"

Lushly oceans, with velvety, liquid light,
These seas that span the universe,
Flecks of lightning, flashes of gold,
Like a billion suns at once explode,
And catch the tiny corner of her sky blue eye...

...She is dancing, see her silver silhouette,
Spinning in her radiance, as she, pirouette,
And catches tiny hollow spheres with iridescent skins,
These translucent bubbles with rash of rainbow tint,
Immersed in the ambient music of the heavens,
That illuminates her soul...

"Kayleigh Beach"

It is timeless in the eternity of the now,
In an uncharted nebula within this archipelago,
Anchored in faith amongst the Exuma Cays,
Rainbow coral reefs breathe,
As pristine pearly aqua waters lap white powder beach,
Blushing ink green currents,
Mix gently into crystal clear tropical waves,
Pouring through the sand bars,
And deep cuts between the dreams,
Constantly shifting light,
Electric cyan pools, refracting saintly,
Heavenly sandbars like vibrant oil paintings,
Stretch off into this range of footprint free dunes,
Expand out under sea salt scented moons,
It is in this chain devoid of human eye,
Among the six score mile long,
Pearly chain of the Out Isles,
Oval intimate lands,
Strung bead by bead and surrounded by turquoise surf,
Hidden from maps and legends,
For the only key to this beach,
Is held by this angel;

This is the beauty of my Daughter,
She reads the depth and the color of the water,
Pinpoints rare shells and thinly scattered sand dollars,
She runs her fingers over the soft bristles of starfish,
And presses her bare feet along the creamy white sand bars,
While walking simultaneously on this broken earth with its scars,
She comes to heal as only she can,
Swimming with schools of French grunts and snapper,
Converses with porcupine pufferfish and queen angelfish,
Who in the shallows gather,
Counting the colors on Caribbean spiny lobsters,
And cradling this beach as a sanctuary for her sea turtles,
A beacon beckoning them home;

She lay on the opaque white sandy beach listening to the melody,
Singing waves of crystal clear water that break on the line,
And echo on a delicate air,
With a perfect sun beaming, she feels the constant temperature of love,
And the soothing, cool ocean breeze that counterbalances the resolve,
Here in Heaven;

She plays in waters of impossible greens and blues,
Swirling with the clouds and sky laced hues,
Under royal purple, gold and green skies,
She gathers all she sees in her radiant sapphire eyes...

...And passes these scenes to me while I sleep.

"The Secret of the Water Road"

Opal foam webbing glistens, as the emerald sea, it pulls,
On the lacy sunset curtains that spread out over the flow,
Of warm tropical waters that draw the sunlight below,
Sparkling against the coral, shining up in purple, dreams and gold,
And wreathed in tranquil waters - I see my daughter's soul,
She is reaching for my spirit as if only she knows,
How to teach her Father,
The secrets of the water road...

...She opens up the sea door,
And through its floral glow,
We swim the loving moons of affection,
That rise within our souls...

"The Transition"

Like the moon and every cycle - rise,
You renew and hold me here,
Like the sun too bright for human eyes,
You are just beyond my fear,
Like the stars that mark the traveler's tide,
You the chart - the ship to steer,
Like the galaxies you plant in my skies,
Are all proof that you are here,
Lighting up a pathway home,
To a higher atmosphere.

"Auroral Bridge of Ocean Blooms"

My Earth bathes in auroral activity,
Storms of red charged particles,
Spiritual electricity,
An atmosphere dares a delicate dance,
And settles softly in your moon blue eyes,
Where the illumination of the centuries glows,
Where the static crackles to the touch,
And oceanic flowers, like aqua dreams,
Spread out into a tapestry of floral blooms,
A blanket of life that rolls upon the turquoise waves,
Gently lapping at my conscience,
And flooring a bridge that leads me to your light.

"Water Wave of Warm Wind"

As if the sun's rays were blankets of water,
Flowing in waves from the hand of my daughter,
Raising the celestial breeze from the sea,
When I feel her wrap her light around me,
She is the air that I breathe,
The golden dream within,
And when she holds me,
She wraps me in water waves of warm wind.

"Fingerprints from Heaven"

And here the box of space and time confines,
The human condition and the human mind,
Fault and fury and folly and faith,
Rattle like nails in a metal cage;

And then the moonlight strikes the glass,
And symbols rise and sparkles dance,
Adorned across the window plain,
Fingerprints from Heaven's domain;

And as dimensions merge through each other,
In that cross section we embrace one another,
For long the love it grows with grace,
And lives beyond all time and space;

And then the wind, it kiss the glass,
Her voice, its strength, through window pass,
We laugh amongst the lush, salty green yield,
That grows within...

...Our endless water fields...

"Body of Stars, Body of Light"

Points of jade golden light,
Crystalline white,
They breathe of the sea,
And dance in the trees,
Where she moves with the breeze,
Like the ocean moves in waves,
She sings to me -

We sit on the rocks as the waters under feet,
Slowly rise to the tidal heartbeat,
Talking, just as we always have,
Having what we have always had,
Faith in this magical love,
That in the now is what it always was;

Each day closer, my human skin,
Wears away and weathers thin,
My body of light kept within,
Will one day be one with the wind,
Like yours, My Love...

"On a Nightly Summer Beach"

Night softly clouds - towers of gray,
A beach blackness - webbed and blush,
Humid summer heated sky,
So wet the air to the touch,
Wind low - and it, hush...

...Flashes in their smoky bellies,
A rage of white fire in jagged flight,
Lightning catches the distant sea,
Alight...

...The stars sparkle across nebulous trails,
As we scan the Milky Way,
And it's glittering tail,
Listen - the waves tumble on the beach,
As night softly clouds roll passed our feet...

"Exuma Infinite"

...And as the luminescence drapes the waves,
A sheet of stars webs the waters face,
Glistening green in sparkling blooms,
Birthed from the heat of a humid moon...

...And she walks and she sings,
Walking a beach I've never seen,
A place no imagination can draw upon,
This beach our families Avalon...

...Exuma Infinite,
I cannot quite envision it,
But I know she scouts its heavenly shores,
For the day of our arrival.

ETHEREAL WATER LIGHT

"She Speaks To Me in Purple"

Liquid wisteria, a lilac flesh of light,
Twined with lace of lavender that blooms in the twilight,
Violet dreams of royal voice is strumming in the night,
She speaks to me in purple,
She brings to me my sight.

"The Tapestry of Souls"

They visit as they may,
Always invited,
Never slighted,
Such love as only this tapestry once woven can hold,
They gather in laughter upon these virgin white powder beaches,
Lifting Exuma higher,
In this tapestry of souls;

My father walks the mornings laughing by her side,
And ancestors frolic happily in this world in which they thrive,
Never more reminded,
That they are never more alive,
With bodies of light joyfully full,
They grace deep honor for my Kayleigh,
In this tapestry of souls.

"Deep In Cerulean Blue Meditation"

Deep in meditation, Daddy,
Follow me through the branches,
See them - right there, tracking through the edges of the mangroves,
Hear the lovely lark of the Zenaida doves,
In their call I find another home,
They sing similarly to those of my little loves of my youth,
Just faster than my morning doves in Cleveland used to do,
Daddy, they feed close to sky blue water,
Swallowing tiny dusty gravel for digestion,
Pecking salt from mineral rich soils,
And praying quite happily for all of us;

The hummingbirds sing to me and me to them,
They are green and gold and flanked with feathered gems,
Their tails, like rudders on the winds, shine a purple black,
These woodstars give in the breeze and spiral in the slack;

My Exuma iguanas, Daddy, sunbathe on xeric limestone,
And sleep within the sandy burrows,
And contemplate eternity on warmish sands,
That shine of milky white bone;

My friends, Daddy, you know how the animals love me so,
I've made all of their arrangements to spend their waking hours on our outpost,
And God, He walks this beach with me,
And the angels of the highest order,
They come to lift me to a place,
Where eternity has no corners.

"And What of the Oceans of Time"

Time - it is liquid, it streams,
Like rivers that flow dream to dream,
But what of this dimension,
To truly live - we must press at the veil, at the seams,
Standing hand in hand in both worlds -

Sunset blend with sunrise,
You, with butterflies in your eyes,
And overflowing with love for me,
Gently combing my spirit with your breath,
And walking through me,
Through these spaces where time cannot forget,
Through the open country of my wounded soul,
Where you plant for your Daddy,
Acres of flowers of pure gold,
To reconcile the grief,
And lifted higher,
I can see,
That time - it is awash like the sea,
With waves that can never tame,
Nor capture you and me.

"Like Waves We Cannot See"

Like waves we cannot see,
Crashing into me,
In a moment the tides, they turn,
In the caldron of this grief;

Like waves we cannot see,
Appearing so suddenly,
Slash across the ocean's face,
And shifting sand,
And deposit its weight inside of me;

A prayer that today's life is worthy of our love,
That today's living is a gift worthy of my daughter,
That today's light was a brilliant gem to gift to my beloved girl...

...If only I could carry you,
Like Footprints, Honey, a moment for you...

...Show me and I shall.

"Breathe You"

I breathe your light,
In deep meditation,
Like breathing in a galaxy's nursery,
A million tiny stars flow in the oxygen,
That sparkle in the channels of my blood,
Glittering like acres of diamonds in the sun...

...Invigorating the wounded soul,
Heavy in its shoes on this earthly domain,
Then a heaving step transforms in flight,
Lifting the spirit like the morning shifts the night,
Back and forth,
Each breath exhaled,
All day long,
Each breath a life,
Each breath from death inhaled.

"Celestial Bird"

The lark that nested in the habitable zone,
An angel that nestled in the hidden gardens on this liquid stone,
And there it reinforced its well-traveled wings,
With fibers twined in utopian fleece,
And filled with love and light and peace,
She wrapped around the moon as Saturn wraps within its rings...

"The Laughter of Artemis"

The crystal bowl in which Artemis gathered light,
Has taken to the wind in lunar flight,
She gathers quivers and strings her bow,
And dances with Orion where the thickets grow;

In the deep gold flesh of her body of light,
She breathes God's love that fills her life,
Just like the dish in which the moon has bathed,
The vessel she is illuminates...

...And deer have come and cypress bend,
And sacred gardens open then,
She laughs, she smiles beneath the glow,
And embraces the moon...

...When it is full.

"Walking a Full Copper Blue Moon"

The Full Moon huddled in the safety of painted, oily waves,
It's droplets of light scatter like fire jewels,
Sprinkling and dusting the tidal aqua pools,
And the rolling fields of the shallows,
With silver flames,
And sparkle on the beachfront with misty water petals,
Where the moist sand absorbs the moon's luminous blaze,
Softly sinking in the sand where our steps are traced,
Where we walk hand in hand,
In a sacred manner,
In this sacred place.

"On Another Planet"

On another beach upon another planet,
Across the plains of magically colored oceans,
Stars sparkle with the illumination of thousands of suns,
Like The Milky Way afire in your palm,
So vibrant you can touch it and taste it,
A morning ocean, quiet calm,
On another planet where expands this beach,
The sands of which are pressed by an angel's feet,
Anxiously awaiting the arrival of her Father,
With giddy laughter and perfect peace...

"Of Another Sky"

And here the air, a scented dream, fills the soul as I pass,
And here I walk upon an ever brittle sheet of flexing glass,
That separates this earth from a higher earth,
One soiled and spiked with light,
And not of sediment and metals and dirt,
Barefoot, I step across the great divide,
With damaged feet and a heavy heart that hurts,
It hurts,
It really hurts...

...My wounded eyes, in aching glance, arch,
Into the burden where space and time collide,
Longing to unclothe my quilted, bloodied, matted wings,
And place them, sacredly,
With purple lilacs and lavender and lilies,
And a prayer,
At the altar on the gold crusted threshold of another sky.

"Walking on Stars"

Lakes of stars pool in the corners of the canthus,
And shoot across the uncharted oceans of our eyes,
Enchanted and ethereal,
A bridge of tears across the skies,
We find each other in our playgrounds of galaxies,
And embrace as deeply as the universe is wide,
We are, together, walking on stars,
The bond of which cannot one divide.

"Light Flesh"

Each pore a star,
A pool of glowing light,
The skin a golden ocean,
That encases brilliant life,
Your eyes illuminate,
You are luminous,
In your lunar grace,
That strikes a blow against the night.

"She Paints the Wild Clouds"

And, indelible, we pry,
Through the halls of waking eye,
In hopes of glance that preys on the darkness,
For we need the breath of light,
For it teaches us, in spite,
Of the moments in this life we find to be heartless -

She rises, and rises - smiling on the halo of the sun,
She paints wild rainbows into the ribcage of clouds,
As the clouds, in their thunder run,
Explode with echoes off into the horizon -

And, incredibly, we try,
Through the halls of drying eyes,
To emerge from the surge of grief and its darkness,
For with this, the bread of life,
We may see, though not with sight,
But with knowledge of the sky,
And the strength to impart this -

She is here - call us to this higher ground,
To where the angels gather round,
Where only love and light and found,
Where she paints the wild clouds for her family...

"We Are Rivers of Living Water"

Stumbling out from under the smoldering vestibule,
Baptized like few, who have been thus challenged, defy,
He emerges as the battle dust settles,
As the death smoke subsides,
A warrior with a wound a moon mile wide,
It weeps like the Word of God from the hole in his side,

'I am coming! I am here! I will find you!'
He cried -

Over mountains where the blue clouds below revive,
And silver rams and rabbits and wild green birds somehow survive,
Through the valleys and rivers and deserts,
And thickets and dreams,
Where the day becomes night,
And the night clings to his wings,
And now fallen, he crawls onward,
Onward toward the soft, green sea -

"Then the angel showed me the river of the water of life,"
As bright as dancing crystals consuming light,
Flowing from the throne of God,
Blazing through the middle of the night,
Exploding into a bouquet of fire flowers,
That ignite your moonlit eyes,
While a bashful earth, its poles upended,
Embarrassed with its floral disguise,
Bows reverently to this one,
As she pushes the equator aside,

"I knew you would come!"
She cried –

And confidently takes center stage,
And radiates as she reaches for his crippled hand,
And with the kiss of life, raises this man,
Her Father, this warrior, this warrior who was,
As fierce in dedication as eternal love,
For his daughter...

...And together,
Out of their sparkling souls...

...Flow rivers of living water...

"Sea Shells of Light"

I see a little girl with wispy, thin blonde hair, in a silky pink nightgown, marching down the beach along the tall profile of a granite, jagged wall, a rock revetment built to hold back the tides; barefoot, she glides along the wet slope between the base of the rocks and the ocean that licks gently at the sand just feet away from her; tiny footprints dot the space behind her, jagging in a soft wavering line; she leans over and snatches little objects and swings her arms back and forth as she picks up the pace, glancing over her shoulder to me ever so often; smiling in her magical, deep blue eyes, fluttering with love for me and spreading her radiance across the morning beach.

Then I see a woman, a tall, thin, young woman walking before me, with full, long, beautiful golden blonde hair, blowing in the sea breeze over her shoulders and dancing in the air beside her; she is wearing a cute, black bikini, proud of who she is; staring at the wet, sandy earth, scanning for treasures, she occasionally stops and sits on her ankles, balancing herself as she picks through the surf and lifts eye catching figures in her fingers; she smiles at me and bats her eyes; she loves me; she is the essence of peace.

I see this little girl, this woman, my little girl woman, now merged together with her every age in one beautiful composition of angelic and stoic golden light, a million points of light embodying her frame, walking the glistening milk white shores of eternity, reaching where I cannot yet reach, walking where I cannot yet walk, gathering little sea shells from the beaches of Heaven and handing them to me; little sparkling shells of blinding light and brilliant love and eternal timeless glorious joy; reaching across the veil of wind in the fullness of her current and present life, and I awake, with eyes and soul and hands open, receive her gifts as she fills my eyes and ears and palms with sea shells illuminated in God's own light.

"Here, Daddy, isn't this one pretty?" she says, "I picked this one just for you," she continues, pauses and smiles, "love you."

"This Angel and the Ocean"

And I, who have been floating,
So many years - or many more,
And my knees now graze lightly,
Upon the bottom of a sandy shore,
Still floating in the currents,
Still floating towards that door,
The tidal shallows father me,
They gather me in gold,
And push me gently like driftwood,
Upon this beach, it's floor,
That stretches out abundantly,
In radiance and light,
She took me by the hand,
To set my feet just right,
And walked me from the water's edge,
That glistened, warm and bright,
And kissed my soul as I stood upon,
The island of new life.

"The Singing Lights"

Passion tears flow from the corners of the lights,
Weeping from the windows in the borders of a starlit night,
Millions of tiny diamonds sparkle,
Stirred up in the water's wake,
Singing in the orchestra of a collapsing wave as it breaks…

…And these shells with the full moon blooming,
And these shells, and the soul it's soothing,
And these shells emit life…

…It is true…

"Higher Sea of White"

I dream to hear with my higher eye,
I breathe to taste with its wider sight,
I see with my soul beyond the mist of human mind,
Aspire to spire and pierce the leather veil of skies;

And there beyond the spirit glows,
Walking opal beachfront dressed in white agate robes,
Upon a seashore with waxy, vitreous tidal ash,
And translucent waters glisten in opaque waves that crash,
Foaming with intense sunlight,
That wash under and over and glisten against her feet,
To the sound of one thousand angels,
Like tiny turquoise bells,
And millions of silver seashells,
That, as one voice, rise, and for her, sing...

"The Wind"

It's pulse - wax and wane,
Finds open window frame,
And breathes its prayer unto me;

The curtains dance on the breeze,
On a sacred melody,
I listen - and then I see...

...Washing the weight from my feet,
Washing away today's grief,
Washing me into its sea,
Where the waters of wind, and time, overtake me...

...Glistening shell on this ethereal beach...

...It took many years to perfect you.

"Blending Souls"

Blend aura flesh,
And spiritual mesh,
Our streams of liquid light,
Weave together thread by thread;

Converge pink and white,
And become golden bright,
More together we are,
Than separate we are less...

...Divinity breathe us - we are home,
We in the blending of souls.

"Skipping Stars"

A bucket full of sea shells,
A pocket full of stars,
She walks on a virgin sand,
That leads to my heart,
She calculates angles,
Like the sea was her art,
And flings the stars like fire coins,
That skip and lift salt water sparks,
Landing in the dream of horizon,
With a splash of lights that leave their marks,
She is painting galaxies...

...By skipping stars.

"Exuma Starlight"

A warmth,
Lore bold,
Usher in oily sky,
Lush, humid aura and salty dust rise,
It glitters, acres of red flash and white spark,
Illuminates the blend as it blunts with blush the dark,
And in the constant splash, emerges a trickling, soft dream,
The waves, with no wind, barely break the seams,
And here I sit with you in the hush,
And I laugh and I cry,
Lost in the warmth and the lore,
Of this starlit sky...

"A Bridge Across the Breach"

A new dawn is cast upon us,
No different, though changing are the roads,
We are growing through transition,
We are taking on different roles,
We are transforming our relationship,
In the sacred beauty of our souls,
For you the light illuminates the everything,
For me, I have before me much growth,
And as the dawn with its morning light,
As the new dawn's sun takes hold,
Our love expands across the breach,
Enriched, empowered, aglow.

"Leaning Into the Next Wave Together..."

Collapse of curled wave,
Explode with a spray,
Just you and me -

As we brace in towards,
The sea's tidal door,
Digging in our feet...

...We lean...

...And the waters recede under knees,
To gather again in the deep,
To gather again to sweep us away,
Yet it never can sweep us away -

And comes the next wave,
To crash in the wake,
Of the last water dream -

Our souls as our tether,
We lean in together,
And tame the wild aqua green sea...

...My Daughter...

...You and me.

"Unbreakable"

Grind shell to sand,
And ancient forest bands,
Emerge across the beach,
Years of flush tides,
Scrape off the eyes,
Like color is touched by bleach,
We walk, untethered, on this sea...

...Tumbling, small stones come to rest,
While ghost crabs tunnel for their nests,
The quiet overcomes you...

...And the heat...

...Trickling waves crash,
They rise and collapse,
And breathe upon the beach,
Leaving tangling seaweed,
And floral debris,
We search for treasures underneath...

...Late afternoon, silence, peace...

...Impressing our prints in the sand,
Smile in gentle laughter,
And miles to walk hand in hand...

...We know.

"Across Angelic Sands"

An orange fire burns in an indigo, auburn sky,
Deep above a turquoise wonderland,
Scarlet bands of misty cloud,
Catch the sun's rays as they expand,
Bowing in the glory of the Mighty One,
Who kneels to take us by the hand,
And walk us through the steps of conscience,
To settle that which we don't understand,
To only emerge with a fresh resolve,
Walking by a glistening turquoise sea...

...In another dimension...

...Across angelic sands.

"Daddy and Daughter Footprints in the Sand"

Beneath blue sky, this turquoise sea, it sighs,
Cresting with purpose,
Like birds of prey,
Above - touch clouds, swoop and glide,
And colors catch in the salted foam webbing of waves,
Light green crystals sparkle,
And melt away in the heat of stunning, sunny, summer day…

…Exuma Infinite, it is perfect in every way;

We were walking - walking there, there in eternal light,
We dared the footsteps that tracked through soft white sands,
From always morning until never night;

The glow it captured us - consuming our words,
And blessing us with a silence that nothing can disturb,
Deep within our hearts,
Where our love is loyal,
It is faithful,
It is eternal,
And ever graceful,
It is Exuma,
It is the sea,
It is Heaven…

…You and me…

www.ingramcontent.com/pod-product-compliance
Lightning Source LLC
Chambersburg PA
CBHW011140290426
44108CB00020B/2699